To Our Parents

TEACH ME ABOUT SALVATION
© 1990 by Linda Sattgast & Jan Elkins
Published by Multnomah Press
Portland, Oregon 97266

Printed in Hong Kong

Library of Congress Cataloging-in-Publication Data

Sattgast, L. J., 1953-
    Teach me about salvation / by L.J. Sattgast and Jan Elkins ; illustrated by Russ Flint.
        p.   cm.
    Summary: A simple explanation of salvation, the concept that Jesus Christ will forgive and save those who believe in him, despite their sins.
    ISBN 0-88070-383-0
    1. Salvation—Juvenile literature. [1. Salvation. 2. Jesus Christ]   I. Elkins, Jan.
II. Flint, Russ, ill. III. Title.
BT751.2.S265   1990
234'.13—dc20   90-35421
                                                                                    CIP
                                                                                    AC

90 91 92 93 94 95 96 97 98 99 - 9 8 7 6 5 4 3 2 1

Teach me about
SALVATION

By L.J. Sattgast & Jan Elkins
Illustrations by Russ Flint

MULTNOMAH
Portland, Oregon 97266

I am a shepherd boy
and this is my little lamb.
I love my lamb, and I take
good care of him.

One day my little lamb ran away.

I called and called for him.

"Where are you, Fluffy?"

But he did not answer.

I looked everywhere for him.

I finally found him—
all dirty and afraid.
I was not mad.
I did not scold.
I hugged him tight and said,
"Oh Fluffy! I love you!"

I took Fluffy home and
gave him a bath.
Now he is all clean
and fluffy again!

I called all my friends and said,
"Look! My little lamb was lost,
but I found him!"
They were happy, too.
"Hurray!" they said.

Parable of the lost sheep (Luke 15:3-7).

I am like a little lamb,
and God is like a shepherd.
Sometimes I disobey, and
sometimes I am not kind
and good. I am lost and
my heart is not clean.

. . . for all have sinned and fall short of the glory of God
(Romans 3:23).

God knew I could never
be good enough by myself.
He knew I was lost
like a little lamb.
So he sent His Son Jesus
to look for his lost sheep.

For God so loved the world that he gave his one and only Son, that whoever believes in him shall not perish but have eternal life (John 3:16).

Some wicked men didn't like
Jesus. They put him on a cross
and killed him.
But Jesus didn't stay dead.
After three days he became
alive again!

. . . that Christ died for our sins according to the Scriptures,
that he was buried, that he was raised on the third day . . .
(1 Corinthians 15:3,4).

Now Jesus is looking for lost
lambs like you and me.

He is not mad.

He does not scold.

Jesus says, "I love you!"

He is patient with you, not wanting anyone to perish,
but everyone to come to repentance (2 Peter 3:9).

Dear Jesus, please forgive me
and wash away all the wrong
things I have done.
Thank you for loving me!

That if you confess with your mouth, "Jesus is Lord,"
and believe in your heart that God raised him from the dead,
you will be saved (Romans 10:9).

Now I belong to God's family.
God is so happy when I believe
in his Son Jesus!
He calls all his angels
to be happy with him!

"... *there is rejoicing in the presence of the angels of God over one sinner who repents*" *(Luke 15:10).*

UNDERSTANDING THE MEANING OF SALVATION

Leading a child to Jesus Christ is a tremendous privilege. You will want to help your child understand these Christian concepts:

- God loves me.
- I have sinned (disobeyed God).
- Jesus died on the cross for my sins.
- God will forgive me, and make me part of his family.

As your child grows, you can elaborate on each of these points, but during the preschool years it is important to keep it simple.

PREPARATION FOR LEADING YOUR CHILD TO CHRIST

- Love your child and be interested in him. If he has a loving relationship with you, it will be easier for him to understand how God loves and cares for him.
- Pray regularly for your child and ask for wisdom. The Holy Spirit will give you nudges as to timing.
- Ask your child leading questions like, "Do you know that Jesus loves you?" If talking about Jesus is a normal part of your conversation, accepting Christ will be a natural step for your child to take.

YOUR CHILD'S READINESS FOR ACCEPTING CHRIST

Can a preschooler ask Jesus to be her Savior? Can a decision made that young be real? If your child has been brought up in a loving home and taught about Jesus, it is not difficult for her to understand God's love at a young age. Children are ready to receive Christ when they:

- Know God loves them.
- Know and agree that they do wrong things.
- Admit without resistance a need for forgiveness.

LEADING YOUR CHILD TO CHRIST

- Pick a time when your child has your full attention. One-on-one is best, since it is easy for children to copy others.

- Explain his need for a Savior. Talk about the wrong things he has done (sin), and then tell him about God's love and forgiveness.
- Ask questions. Don't assume she understands just from listening to your explanation. Take the time to clear up any misconceptions—a couple of days or weeks if necessary.
- Help your child pray one phrase at a time:
    > Jesus, you love me.
    > I want to become a part of your family.
    > I want you to be my Savior.
    > Wash away all the wrong things I have done.
    > Thank you for forgiving me and loving me.

CAUTION
- Use terminology that a child understands.
- Don't try to motivate with pressure or fear. Giving your child time to think about accepting Christ will help take away any feeling of being pressured.
- Don't expect a perfect child in your household because she has accepted the Lord. Change is a process of time and choice.

FOLLOW-UP ON SALVATION
- Have your child tell one or two others about his decision to accept Jesus as his Savior.
- Read the Bible and pray with your child daily. Explain to him that God's Holy Spirit lives in him so he can:
    > Know what is right and wrong.
    > Talk to God anytime and anywhere.
    > Tell others about Jesus.
    > Know that God is always with him.
    > Serve God and others.
- Take advantage of spontaneous opportunities to teach spiritual principles.
- Attend a church that believes in and teaches the Bible.